Our Land, Australia

Written and illustrated by Amy Krieger

© AMY KRIEGER 2023

The **outback** of Australia,
with unique animals far and wide.

If you want to learn more about them,
come on and peek inside…

Snakes lurk amongst the rocks, waiting for their **prey.**

They strike as fast as lightning bolts, their food often can't get away.

Kangaroos are large **marsupials**, they can leap so very high.

With hind legs and a strong tail, they are quick to hop on by.

Cockatoos are the noisy birds, with a **crest** upon their head.

Flying around in large **flocks**, feathers of white, black and red.

The emus are the ones to watch, they're speedy on their feet.

Don't go near their babies though,
they chase and won't retreat.

Furry brown wombats,
are **native** to Aussie land.

They snooze throughout the day,
and dig their **burrows** in the sand.

Platypus are unique creatures, they like to swim in creeks.

Laying eggs to have their babies,
with unusual duck-like beaks.

Echidnas are a special kind, backs full of spikey **quills.**

Always on the hunt for ants,
marching around the rocky hills.

Kookaburras are the laughing birds,
a sound so full of glee.

Keeping a watchful eye on food,
while flying from tree to tree.

Crocodiles are the crafty ones, they have sharp, pointy teeth.

Stalking their unaware **prey**, hiding in murky water beneath.

Koalas are the cuddly bears, eating **eucalyptus** snacks.

Sleeping all throughout the day,
babies clinging to their backs.

Glossary

Burrow: a hole or tunnel created by an animal, used for shelter, sleeping and housing babies

Crest: head feathers on some species of birds that can be raised and lowered depending on mood

Eucalyptus: a specific type of Australian tree

Flock: a group of birds

Marsupial: a mammal that when born, is predominantly carried around in the pouch of its mother

Native: to be born or raised in a specific country or region

Outback: parts of remote Australia, far away from heavily populated towns and cities

Prey: an animal that other animals hunt to eat

Quill: the pointy spikes on echidnas

Special Mentions...

'Our Land, Australia' was edited by Shane Tranter.
Shane, thank you again for your hard work!

Thank you to Roz, my mother, for sharing my writing joy and achievements along my literary journey.

Get in touch!

Email
amy.b.krieger@gmail.com

Follow on Instagram
@by_amy_krieger

© AMY KRIEGER 2023

About the Author/Illustrator

Amy Krieger is a schoolteacher who lives in a beautiful seaside town on the Mornington Peninsula in Victoria, Australia. When Amy is not teaching or writing, she enjoys poetry, drawing and being in the outdoors. Her greatest achievement is being 'mum' to her three beautiful girls, Evie, Gracie and Hallie. They are the sunshine in her life.

Amy loves using nature to draw inspiration for her writing and art pieces, especially with Australian flora and fauna.

Amy and her family love to keep active. They are very much a 'sport obsessed' family, enjoying all things football, netball and cricket. Amy's family including her siblings, own and operate a Brazilian jiu jitsu club on the Mornington Peninsula, *Dromana Grappling Academy*. The ethos of jiu jitsu filters down into their everyday lives of enjoying life, while keeping physically and mentally healthy.

Amy is an up-and-coming author, focusing on writing children's books with positive, meaningful messages for her audience. Her book illustrations are all personally hand-drawn using a mix of modern and traditional art techniques.

Amy is currently working on many new titles. These will be added to her collection in the near future.